DATE DUE

Jacques Cousteau
Conserving Underwater Worlds

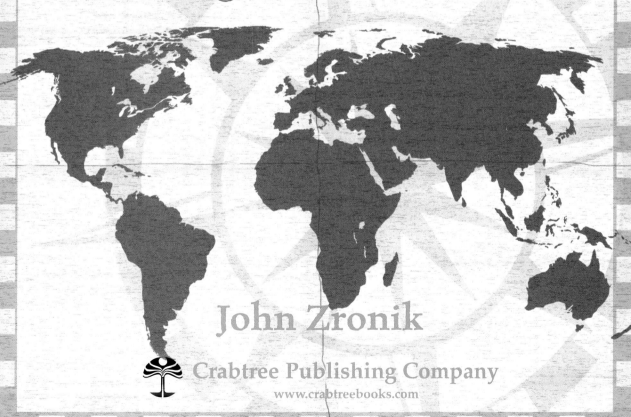

John Zronik

Crabtree Publishing Company
www.crabtreebooks.com

Crabtree Publishing Company

www.crabtreebooks.com

To Bobby — Keeping his head above water more than 40 years

Coordinating editor: Ellen Rodger
Series editor: Carrie Gleason
Editors: Adrianna Morganelli, L. Michelle Nielsen
Design and production coordinator: Rosie Gowsell
Cover design and production assistance: Samara Parent
Art direction: Rob MacGregor
Photo research: Allison Napier
Prepress technician: Nancy Johnson

Photo Credits: PopperfotoAlamy: p. 15; Travelfile/Alamy: p. 13 (bottom); AP Photo: p. 11, p. 31 (bottom); AP Photo/Lionel Cironneau: p. 31 (top); AP Photo/Manuel Lazcano/Jean-Michel Cousteau Productions: p. 30 (top); Tony Arruza/Corbis: p. 25 (top); Tobias Bernhard/zefa/Corbis: p. 20; Bettmann/Corbis: p. 14; Natalie

Fobes/Corbis: p. 19; CP/Everett Collection: cover, p.12, p. 16, p. 22; Getty Images/Cousteau Society: p. 27; The Granger Collection: p. 23, p. 26, p. 29; Jacques Boyer/Roger-Viollet/The Image Works: p. 9; Mary Evans Picture Library/The Image Works: p. 7; The Kobal Collection: p. 10 (bottom), p. 13 (top), p. 21; Peter Scoones/Photo Researchers, Inc.: p. 30 (bottom); Other images from Stock CD.

Cover: Jacques Cousteau was an underwater explorer and a celebrity. Cousteau's hundreds of books, films, and television programs brought the ocean world to people living on land.

Sidebar icon: Cousteau encountered many different types of tropical fish on his voyages.

Library and Archives Canada Cataloguing in Publication

Zronik, John Paul, 1972-
 Jacques Cousteau : conserving underwater worlds / John Zronik.

(In the footsteps of explorers)
Includes index.
ISBN 978-0-7787-2419-3 (bound)
ISBN 978-0-7787-2455-1 (pbk.)

 1. Cousteau, Jacques Yves--Juvenile literature.
2. Oceanographers--France--Biography--Juvenile literature.
I. Title. II. Series.

GC30.C68Z76 2007   j551.46092   C2007-900664-7

Library of Congress Cataloging-in-Publication Data

Zronik, John Paul, 1972-
 Jacques Cousteau : conserving underwater worlds / written by John Zronik.
  p. cm. -- (In the footsteps of explorers)
 Includes index.
 ISBN-13: 978-0-7787-2419-3 (rlb)
 ISBN-10: 0-7787-2419-0 (rlb)
 ISBN-13: 978-0-7787-2455-1 (pb)
 ISBN-10: 0-7787-2455-7 (pb)
  1. Cousteau, Jacques Yves.--Juvenile literature. 2. Oceanographers--France--Biography--Juvenile literature. I. Title. II. Series.

GC30.C68Z76 2007
551.46092--dc22
[B]   2007003405

Crabtree Publishing Company

Published in Canada
Crabtree Publishing
616 Welland Ave.
St. Catharines, ON
L2M 5V6

Published in the United States
Crabtree Publishing
PMB16A
350 Fifth Ave., Suite 3308
New York, NY 10118

Published in the United Kingdom
Crabtree Publishing
White Cross Mills
High Town, Lancaster
LA1 4XS

Published in Australia
Crabtree Publishing
386 Mt. Alexander Rd.
Ascot Vale (Melbourne)
VIC 3032

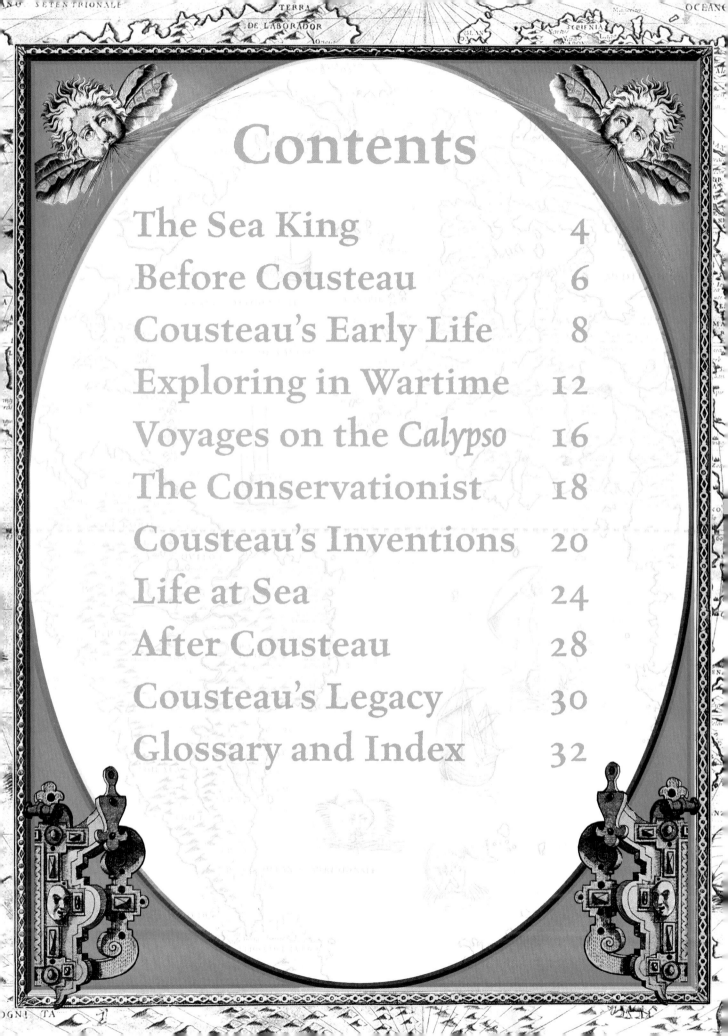

Contents

The Sea King 4

Before Cousteau 6

Cousteau's Early Life 8

Exploring in Wartime 12

Voyages on the *Calypso* 16

The Conservationist 18

Cousteau's Inventions 20

Life at Sea 24

After Cousteau 28

Cousteau's Legacy 30

Glossary and Index 32

The Sea King

Jacques Cousteau is one of history's most famous undersea explorers. Born in 1910, Cousteau became a scientist, writer, researcher, sailor, inventor, filmmaker, and television star. Cousteau made it his mission to educate people about the world below the surface of the Earth's oceans.

Cousteau thought of the Earth as a "water planet," and spent most of his life exploring its seas and the plants and animals that live in them.

Cousteau's Inventions

Cousteau helped develop inventions that allowed people to explore the oceans as they never had before. Among these inventions was the Aqua-Lung, which allowed humans to move and breathe freely under water for long periods of time. Cousteau also helped develop underwater film and video equipment, submarines used for exploration, and structures that allowed humans to live under the sea for weeks at a time. These inventions helped expand people's knowledge about the ocean and inspired future generations of undersea explorers.

Sending a Message

Through his films, books, and television shows, Cousteau made millions of people see that the Earth's overall health is connected to the health of its oceans. Cousteau filmed more than one hundred television programs and published dozens of books during his life. During the 1960s and 1970s, he was the host of a popular TV series about ocean life. Cousteau showed people how activities such as mining and **oil drilling** could be dangerous to the oceans.

In His Own Words

Jacques Cousteau first became fascinated by the underwater world during the 1930s, while stationed on the shores of the Mediterranean Sea as a member of the French Navy. Later in life, Cousteau wrote about the mysterious world he had discovered below the surface of the water during that time, a world he knew was waiting to be explored.

"There beneath the keels of our boats lies a little-known yet penetrable universe teeming with life - a wild marine jungle separated from our civilized world only by the surface of the sea, an ever changing boundary that conceals the world below from our eyes and has enveloped her in mystery and legend."

- Jacques Cousteau

(below) Cousteau's work helped make underwater exploration possible. Today, many people put on SCUBA diving gear and explore *coral reefs*.

- 1910 -
Cousteau is born in Saint-Andre-de-Cubzac, France.

- 1933 -
Cousteau joins the French Navy.

- 1943 -
Cousteau helps invent the Aqua-Lung.

- 1950 -
Cousteau acquires the *Calypso*, the ship he uses for most of his life.

- 1953 -
Cousteau publishes *The Silent World*, **a book that sold five million copies.**

Before Cousteau

The planet's oceans, the Pacific, Atlantic, Indian, and Arctic, are all connected to each another. As well as oceans, the Earth holds many smaller saltwater seas, including the Caribbean Sea and Mediterranean Sea. Little was known about life in the world's oceans and seas before Cousteau's expeditions.

Free Divers

Before humans had equipment that allowed them to breathe under water, they were limited to diving as deep as they could while holding their breath. People used this method of diving to harvest food, pearls, and sponges from the sea. These divers faced dangers, including jellyfish, sharks, and drowning.

(below) Before the Aqua-Lung, undersea divers were confined to walking on the ocean floor in bulky diving suits and helmets.

Ocean Pioneer

During the late 1800s, a Scottish scientist named Charles Wyville Thomson had an idea for a sea voyage that would change the way humans looked at the world's oceans. Thomson **modified** a British Navy ship and used it for the purpose of studying the seas. Thomson and his partners built laboratories onboard the ship before setting out to observe ocean life. Thomson and fellow scientists discovered more than 4,000 new animal species.

The Miller Dunn Helmet

In 1916, the American Miller Dunn Company began selling a helmet that allowed divers to breathe while exploring shallow waters. Divers could not move freely under water while using the helmet, but were confined to walking on the ocean floor. The Miller Dunn helmet was made from copper and had a six-inch (15-cm) round, clear faceplate that allowed divers to see. Air was pumped to divers though a tube on a ship or on land.

(background) Early underwater explorers and inventors developed devices to aid in exploring the seas. This illustration shows a bathysphere developed by American Otis Barton in 1930. The mythical sea creatures show how much people did not know of undersea life at that time. Even today new sea animals are still being discovered.

Cousteau's Early Life

Jacques Cousteau was born in Saint Andre de Cubzac, a small town in southwest France, in 1910. Cousteau's father, Daniel Cousteau, was a lawyer. His mother, Elizabeth, worked caring for the family.

The Birth of an Explorer

When Jacques was a young boy, his father worked for a wealthy American businessman named Eugene Higgins. The Cousteaus often traveled with Higgins to his waterfront properties or on his yacht, where young Jacques became accustomed to the ocean. In 1920, the Cousteaus moved to New York, where Higgins required the services of Jacques' father. During Cousteau's time in the United States, Jacques went to summer camp in Vermont. There, he often swam in the lake, proving himself a good swimmer. A camp councilor noticed Jacques' talent for swimming and asked him to clear branches from the bottom of the lake. Jacques learned to hold his breath under water as he performed the task.

With his camera, Cousteau captured images of distant lands and cultures.

Growing Up

By the time Jacques was thirteen years old, his family had moved back to France. Cousteau bought one of the first "motion picture" cameras sold in Paris and began making movies of his family. After graduation, Cousteau attended the naval academy and entered the French Navy in 1933. He was stationed at Brest, on the northern coast of France. Cousteau traveled the world serving as a gunnery officer and took his motion picture camera with him. Making these early movies gave Cousteau experience he would use in his future career as a professional filmmaker.

Grounded by Accident

A gunnery officer's job is to care for and maintain **ammunition** onboard a naval ship. Gunnery officers are also responsible for the launching and recovery of Navy aircraft. While serving as a gunnery officer, Cousteau entered the navy's aviation school, where pilots were trained. Soon after beginning this training, Cousteau suffered injuries in a car accident that ended his flying career. He was the only person in a car that traveled off the road and crashed. Cousteau's left arm was broken in five places and his right arm was so infected he could not move it. Doctors recommended that Cousteau have the arm **amputated**, but Cousteau refused. He worked to recover from the accident for a year, swimming to regain his strength. The injuries left Cousteau unable to resume flight training, so he was assigned to duty at the port of Toulon, France, on the Mediterranean Sea.

(below) A French navy ship in the Port of Toulon during World War I (1914-1918). Cousteau was stationed at Toulon during World War II.

Seeing the Sea

While stationed at Toulon, Cousteau met Philippe Tailliez and Frederic Dumas, who would become his trusted diving companions. In 1936, Cousteau and Tailliez tested a pair of underwater goggles near the port. After looking under the water and seeing an abundance of life, Cousteau felt his future was tied to the sea. "Sometimes we are lucky enough to know that our lives have been changed," he said after the experience. "It happened to me that summer's day, when my eyes were opened on the sea."

(above) Many of Cousteau's family members grew up to make films and raise awareness of ocean animals. Jean-Michel made a film called Sharks 3D.

Jacques Cousteau with his oldest son, Jean-Michel, who was born in 1938. Cousteau's second son, Philippe, was born in 1940. Both sons spent time with their father and mother on expeditions, learning to dive and studying sea life.

(background) In 1937, Cousteau married Simone Melchior, who would become a partner in his future adventures. She was the first woman to dive using the Aqua-Lung and became a mother-like figure to Cousteau's crew during 40 years of ocean exploration.

Exploring in Wartime

Jacques Cousteau's early work exploring under water took place during World War II. By 1940, Germany occupied parts of France. As the war was being fought, Cousteau worked developing his most famous invention.

The Aqua-Lung

In 1943, Cousteau and **engineer** Emile Gagnon invented the Aqua-Lung. Cousteau wanted to create a device that allowed humans to swim freely while being able to breathe under water. He also wanted to ensure divers had the correct amount of oxygen during their dives. Equipment before the Aqua-Lung could send too much oxygen into a diver's blood stream, causing them to become ill. The invention of the Aqua-Lung was also useful in the French war effort, allowing divers to inspect and repair ships while under water.

Testing the Invention

Cousteau made his first dives using the Aqua-Lung in the Mediterranean Sea, off the coast of France, during 1943. That summer, Cousteau made 500 dives with the new invention, taking underwater photographs of what he saw below the water's surface. Cousteau and his diving companions tested the limits of the Aqua-Lung, going more than 200 feet (61 meters) under the sea. Cousteau also used the Aqua-Lung to make underwater movies. Cousteau showed a French **admiral** and his staff the underwater film and was ordered to begin underwater experiments for the Navy.

A movie poster for one of Cousteau's later underwater films, The Silent World.

This more recent photograph shows Cousteau wearing later SCUBA diving equipment. The Aqua-Lung Cousteau helped develop allowed him to be a "manfish," or to breathe under water.

How It Worked

The Aqua-Lung automatically fed divers **compressed** air from cylinders strapped to their backs. A device called a **regulator** was used to control the flow of air to the diver. Two tubes extending from the regulator attached to a **mouthpiece** that was used to breathe while under water. A watertight mask covered a diver's nose and eyes, and allowed the diver to see. Flippers strapped to the divers' feet helped them move through the sea. The Aqua-Lung was modeled after a device conceived in 1925 by Captain Yves Le Prieur. Le Prieur's invention provided a diver with a continuous flow of compressed air, unlike the Aqua-Lung's regulated flow. Using a continuous flow of air, the amount of time a diver could spend under water was limited. Today, the Aqua-Lung is better known as SCUBA gear. The word SCUBA stands for Self-Contained Underwater Breathing Apparatus.

Flippers are part of the gear of SCUBA divers.

Undersea Research Group

After receiving his orders, Cousteau formed the Undersea Research Group, a branch of the French Navy. The group, which included Dumas and Tailliez, was given an office in the harbor at Toulon, France. Starting with just two Aqua-Lungs, the Undersea Research Group was soon provided more resources, including ships to use during its missions. The French Navy also provided the group with technical experts, who helped build new and better diving masks, suits, and underwater lighting equipment.

French General Charles de Gaulle addressing French sailors in 1943. Cousteau worked with the French Navy during World War II.

Military Musketeers

The Undersea Research Group was given many missions by the French Navy. Its first assignment was to remove two torpedoes from a sunken German submarine off the coast of France. The group later helped recover unexploded German **mines**. Cousteau and his colleagues also used Aqua-Lungs to make films of submarines traveling under water, which gave military officials a view they had never seen before. The group continued to test the effects of the **depths** on humans, always striving to dive deeper under the sea. For their daring work, Cousteau, Dumas, and Tailliez became known as the "*mousquemers*," or "musketeers of the sea."

Underground Resistance

During World War II, Cousteau was an active member of the French Resistance against the Germans. The French Resistance was made up of different underground, or secret, groups that worked to **undermine** German power. They tried to discover military secrets that could help defeat the German army and its **allies** to free France from German **occupation**. Cousteau took photographs of secret documents after sneaking into an office used by the Italian Navy. For this work, Cousteau was awarded the *Legion d'Honneur*, France's highest military honor.

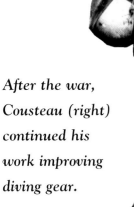

After the war, Cousteau (right) continued his work improving diving gear.

- September, 1939 -
World War II
breaks out
in Europe.

- June 1940 -
Germany occupies
parts of France. By
1942, Germany
occupied the
whole country.

- 1944 -
France begins to
be liberated, or
freed, from
German
occupation,
starting
with Paris.

- 1945 -
Cousteau's
underwater movie
about shipwrecks
is released.

Voyages on the *Calypso*

When Jacques Cousteau left the French Navy in 1950, he was determined to continue exploring the world's oceans. The same year he ended his military service, Cousteau found the ship he would use for this work, the *Calypso*.

Cousteau with some of the artifacts discovered on an ancient shipwreck. The items included ceramic pots, dishes, and jars used to hold wine and olive oil.

First Voyage

The *Calypso*'s first voyage began on November 24, 1951. Cousteau's wife and sons, his friend Dumas, and a crew including divers, scientists, and sailors departed from Toulon, France, for the Red Sea to study coral reefs off the coast of Saudi Arabia. The deep and warm Red Sea contains the perfect conditions for the formation of coral reefs and supports an almost endless abundance of sea life. Cousteau hoped to learn more about the sea's colorful corals and other marine species.

Early Adventures

In 1952, Cousteau and the *Calypso*'s crew went out in search of sunken ships and made a remarkable discovery. About 12 miles (19 km) off the coast of Marseilles, France, near an island called Grand Congloue, the crew discovered a sunken Roman cargo ship dating to about 230 B.C., the oldest ever found. The ship was found in about 150 feet (46 meters) of water. Cousteau and his crew used special underwater vacuums to remove silt and debris from the ship, and salvaged items from the wreck.

Continuing Adventures

Cousteau made hundreds of voyages aboard the *Calypso* during a more than 40-year time span. During the 1960s and 1970s, the *Calypso* and its crew traveled the Atlantic, Pacific, and Indian oceans, the Aegean and Red seas, as well as some of the world's biggest rivers, including the Amazon, Nile, Mississippi, and St. Lawrence. In each of these areas, Cousteau and his crew studied and filmed marine life and environments. In 1985, the *Calypso* was part of a five-year expedition called "rediscovery of the world," which aimed to collect information about the environmental health of the Earth.

Growing Popularity

While onboard the *Calypso*, Cousteau kept a journal of his discoveries and activities that took place on the ship. From his journals, he wrote many articles about his adventures for American magazines during the 1950s. In 1953, Cousteau published *The Silent World*, a book that was translated into 22 languages and sold five million copies. The book helped make Cousteau a popular figure. Cousteau later worked with French film director Louis Malle to produce a feature-length film also called *The Silent World*. Released in 1955, *The Silent World* helped make Cousteau a celebrity and was the first underwater film made in color. The film showed dazzling underwater life in the Mediterranean Sea, the Red Sea, and Persian Gulf, from coral reefs to sharks and whales.

Some of the ocean species Cousteau studied were colored groupers, squid (above), sea turtles (bottom left), manta rays (top), as well as eels (below), sharks, and countless other ocean animals.

The Conservationist

Through his explorations, Jacques Cousteau helped people understand more about the Earth's ecosystem. An ecosystem is a system of relationships among living things. Cousteau showed that the health of people on Earth is related to the health of the planet's oceans.

Saving the Oceans

As part of his work, Cousteau took action to help save the world's oceans. In 1960, the French government planned to allow an energy company to dump tons of **nuclear waste** into the ocean. The plan worried Cousteau, who knew the dangerous material would harm sea life. Cousteau led a public education campaign to stop the dumping and the French government eventually cancelled its plans. Cousteau soon realized it would take an organized effort to save the environment. In 1974, he created The Cousteau Society for this purpose. The society's slogan was "To know, to love, to protect" the Earth's natural environment.

(background) Cousteau knew that if life in the ocean around Antarctica was harmed, then other living things elsewhere would suffer. Cousteau taught people about the environment and led many people to want to protect it.

In 1989, the worst oil spill in American history took place in Alaska. An oil tanker spilled its contents into the Pacific Ocean, affecting marine life. Jacques Cousteau and his son Jean-Michel made a film about the event called Alaska: Outrage at Valdez.

Important Voice

In 1990, Cousteau launched a worldwide petition campaign to save Antarctica, the world's southernmost continent, from mining and oil drilling. Antarctica is home to animals that rely on the ocean for survival, including penguins and other rare species of birds and fish. Cousteau's campaign to save Antarctica was successful. The world's countries agreed to protect the continent for at least 50 years. In 1992, Cousteau was invited to address the **United Nations** Conference on Development and the Environment in Rio de Janeiro, Brazil. He asked world leaders to take immediate action to save the environment. "Future generations would not forgive us for having deliberately spoiled their last opportunity and the last opportunity is today," Cousteau said at the time.

- 1985 -
Cousteau receives the U.S. Presidential Medal of Freedom.

- 1988 -
Cousteau is placed on the United Nations roll of honor of environmental protection.

- 1988 -
Cousteau is awarded the National Geographic Society's centennial award.

- 1992 -
Cousteau participates in the UN Conference on Development and the Environment in Brazil.

Cousteau's Inventions

Throughout his life, Jacques Cousteau helped develop inventions that increased human knowledge about the world's oceans. These inventions included diving and film equipment, as well as undersea homes and vehicles.

Underwater Pictures

Cousteau helped develop inventions that improved underwater film technology. In the 1950s, Cousteau worked onboard the *Calypso* developing new underwater photography equipment with crew member Luis Marden. The equipment included new cameras, filters, lenses, and lighting for underwater filming. In 1963, Cousteau helped develop an underwater camera known as the "Calypso-Phot." This camera technology was later sold to Nikon, a large camera company. Cousteau's work developing underwater film equipment helped bring the world under the ocean to movie and television screens for the first time.

Today there are many underwater photographers.

A scene from Cousteau's film, World Without Sun, *which was about Conshelf II. The Conshelf project helped prove humans could live and work under the ocean for long periods of time.*

The Conshelf Project

During the 1960s, Cousteau planned the Conshelf project, which would allow humans to live under the ocean for weeks at a time. In 1962, Cousteau and his team built Conshelf I, a dome-shaped structure 33 feet (10 meters) below the ocean's surface, off the coast of France. Two divers, Albert Falco and Claude Wesly, lived for a week inside Conshelf I, leaving the structure to explore the ocean floor using Aqua-Lungs. During the summer of 1963, Cousteau developed Conshelf II, which was also known as "starfish house." The structure included sleeping space, a kitchen, lab, and photography room.

Undersea Living

Five divers lived for a month in Conshelf II, 36 feet (11 meters) below the ocean's surface. Conshelf II also included a "deep cabin," where two divers lived 85 feet (26 meters) under water. Later, Cousteau built Conshelf III, where divers lived for one month 325 feet (100 meters) below the surface. The Conshelf projects allowed divers more time to explore and research because they did not have to go through decompression when they returned to the surface. Decompression is when a diver makes stops along the way back to the surface, allowing the body to adjust to **pressure** changes at different depths.

- 1959 -
The *SP-350* diving saucer, or *Denise*, is launched.

- 1962 -
Conshelf I is set up off the coast of France, in the Mediterranean Sea.

- 1963 -
Conshelf II is built on the floor of the Red Sea.

- 1965 -
Conshelf III is set up off the coast of Nice, France.

- 1967 -
Two *SP-500s*, or *Sea Fleas*, are launched.

Cousteau explains how one of his submersibles works in this photograph. By conducting observations from Sea Fleas, *scientists were able to gain a better understanding of underwater ecosystems.*

Sea Fleas

In 1967, Cousteau launched two underwater vehicles called *Sea Fleas*. These small **submersibles** were designed for underwater exploration and observation. Two *Sea Fleas* were developed, called the *SP-500s*. They were based on an earlier design, the smaller *SP-350*. Both were saucer-shaped vehicles. *Sea Fleas* were used for filming under water and had mechanical arms that enabled explorers to grab objects under the ocean's surface.

The Turbosail

In 1980, Cousteau, along with Professor Lucien Malavard and engineer Bertrand Charrier, designed a new wind-power system for boats called the Turbosail. The Turbosail was an engine system partly powered by the wind. When Cousteau launched a new ship called the *Alcyone* in 1985, it was equipped with two Turbosails. The Turbosail helped power the ship using the combination of a modern engine and wind. When sailing in strong winds, a Turbosail would provide power, requiring less use of a ship's mechanical engine. The Turbosail provided a clean, renewable source of power, meaning less use of oil-burning engines, which pollute the environment.

Cousteau climbs into the SP-350, or Denise. The diving saucer held two people who laid on mattresses and looked out the portholes while under water.

The ship Jacques Cousteau sailed for more than 40 years exploring the world's oceans was called the *Calypso.* Cousteau's family and closest friends were a part of the *Calypso's* crew.

Dedicated Crew

Each crew member onboard the *Calypso* was dedicated to the ship's mission: to explore and learn more about the world's oceans. The crew became a family, sharing a love for the sea. Crew members and divers worked hard, often day and night in all kinds of weather. Along with their scientific duties, crew members were responsible for routine daily maintenance and emergency repairs. Each crew member pitched in with cleaning and chores. All of the crew's hard work paid off, as Cousteau and his divers went to depths not reached before and discovered countless natural wonders below the surface of the ocean. During the *Calypso's* many voyages, its crew size varied depending on the mission it was undertaking.

Cousteau's Ship

The *Calypso* measured 139 feet (42 meters) long. With its two engines running, it traveled at a top speed of ten knots. The ship included a mess hall where the crew ate, a radio room for communications equipment, an engine room to power the ship, a steering room to control it, as well as a kitchen, walk-in freezer, storage areas, washroom, and showers. Crew members slept in cabins onboard the ship. At the front of the *Calypso*, an underwater observation chamber allowed for viewing under the surface of the ocean. A crane on the ship's deck was used for lifting diving equipment and other supplies on and off the ship. The *Calypso* was also equipped with storage tanks for fuel, oil, and fresh water.

> *Conshelf structures provided divers living under the sea with air, water, food, and electricity. While living beneath the ocean, divers kept busy performing scientific experiments and underwent medical exams to monitor their health.*

Fun and Games
The *Calypso's* crew worked hard, but also took time to have fun. Crew members had contests for the funniest hat and even placed flying fish into fellow crew members beds to give them a night-time scare.

Grilled Seafood Shish Kebabs
Try this tasty *Calypso* seafood treat. Ask an adult for help.

Ingredients: (amounts vary depending on size of group)
Shelled shrimp
Fresh scallops
Halibut cut into one-inch cubes
Red pepper cut into one-inch squares
Green pepper cut into one-inch squares
   Melted butter
      Shish kabob skewers

Directions:
1. Place ingredients on skewers.
2. Melt butter.
3. Coat ingredients on skewers with melted butter.
4. Cook over grill on high heat for 10 minutes, turning often. Coat ingredients with butter during cooking. The skewers are finished cooking when the halibut turns white.

Driving the Ship

Cousteau was in charge of the *Calypso's* scientific and research missions, but operating the ship was left to the crew. The *Calypso's* first official captain and pilot was Francois Saout, a long-distance sailboat racer. Albert Falco later became captain and chief diver of the *Calypso*. The *Calypso's* captain used navigation equipment, including **sonar**, **radar**, and automatic steering, to pilot the ship. To maintain contact with the outside world, the *Calypso* was equipped with radios, telephones, and fax machines. The ship also had a chief engineer, who ensured the ship's machinery ran well.

Scientific Cargo

The *Calypso* carried cargo used for scientific purposes. Diving equipment, including regulators, tanks, suits, belts, and fins, had their own storage area. So did film and photography equipment, including lights and cameras. A helicopter called "Felix," which Cousteau acquired to help in his scientific work and filmmaking, was stored on a platform at the back of the ship's deck. Underwater vehicles, including *Sea Fleas*, were kept near the *Calypso's* crane, also at the back of the ship. The *Calypso* was also equipped with a scientific laboratory.

(top right) Captain Cousteau at the controls of the helicopter, "Felix." The equipment needed for the ocean research done by Cousteau and his crew was expensive. Cousteau spent much of the time trying to get funding for their work.

The *Calypso*

The *Calypso*, formerly named J-826, was originally a minesweeper, a type of ship used to remove mines from the water during and after World War II. Cousteau saw the ship as an ideal vessel to modify for ocean exploration and diving work, but could not afford to buy the ship. Cousteau contacted a wealthy English naturalist named Loel Guinness, who also had a passion for knowing more about the oceans. Guinness agreed to purchase the *Calypso* and lend it to Cousteau to use during his explorations. Cousteau made renovations to the ship, installing scientific equipment, underwater windows for observation, and a lookout deck.

The Cousteau fleet: Felix (above), the Calypso (right), and the Alcyone (far right).

After Cousteau

Jacques Cousteau died on June 25, 1997. He is remembered for his work helping protect the environment and for the many inventions he helped develop.

- 1979 -
Cousteau's son, Philippe, is killed in a plane crash.

- 1990 -
Cousteau's first wife, Simone, dies of cancer.

- 1991 -
Cousteau marries for a second time, to Francine Triplet.

- 1997 -
Cousteau dies of a heart attack at the age of 87.

Ocean Pioneer

Cousteau was a pioneer of ocean exploration. His work opened the undersea world to future generations. The scientific research team he led on the *Calypso* showed people how the health of oceans affect the overall health of the Earth. Cousteau's work to prevent the dumping of nuclear waste, preserve Antarctica, and create a greater respect for the planet has inspired other people to save the Earth's environment. Many have formed organizations that aim to protect the world's natural areas. Cousteau also inspired students at universities around the world to study oceans and the life they contain.

Scientific Research

Cousteau made many contributions to the world of science. These included the Aqua-Lung, underwater vehicles for scientific exploration, and improved diving equipment and underwater cameras. Cousteau's inventions opened the world underwater to human exploration, allowing people to study ocean creatures and habitats as they never had before. All of this new equipment also helped in Cousteau's effort to teach people about marine plant and animal life. Cousteau's pioneering work in underwater photography and film opened a new world to future filmmakers and television producers.

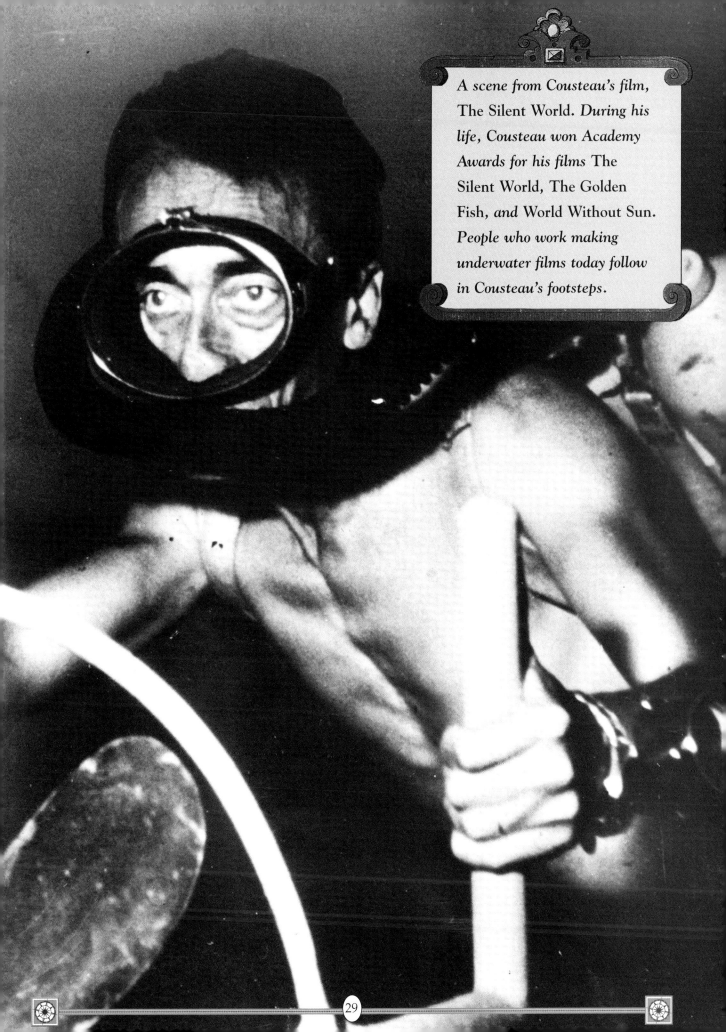

A scene from Cousteau's film, The Silent World. *During his life, Cousteau won Academy Awards for his films The Silent World, The Golden Fish, and World Without Sun. People who work making underwater films today follow in Cousteau's footsteps.*

Cousteau's Legacy

Jacques Cousteau's work continues to have an impact on the world today. The Cousteau Society, an organization Cousteau started to help preserve the environment, today has 15,000 members and works to protect the Earth.

Continuing Tradition

Cousteau's family continues his mission today. Cousteau's son, Jean-Michel, and grandson, Fabien, are both involved in work to protect the environment. Fabien Cousteau, is also an undersea explorer, and studies sharks. Fabien designed a submarine called the Trojan Shark, in the shape of a great white shark. Philippe Cousteau Jr., Jacques Cousteau's grandson, also works studying and making films about the oceans.

(below) Bleached coral in the Indian Ocean. Scientists believe global warming, caused by pollution, may be the cause.

(above) Jean-Michel Cousteau runs the Ocean Futures Society, a non-governmental, marine conservation and education organization.

Still Threatened

Despite the work of Cousteau and others to preserve the environment, human activities still threaten the planet. Many species of marine animals have been protected and preserved, but many are still at risk. Today, Antarctica is threatened by **global warming** and pollution continues to affect ocean life around the world.

(left) Children view an exhibit of Cousteau's diving suit at the Oceanographic Institute and Museum in Monaco, where Cousteau was Director from 1957 to 1988. Cousteau's television shows and books were loved by children around the world.

Environmental Celebrity

Many of Cousteau's 100 television programs brought public awareness to environmental problems. People listened to Cousteau's message in part because he was a likable character. With his soft French accent and trademark red wool hat, Cousteau made a connection with viewers. He is remembered as one of television's best and most likable documentary makers.

The cover of Cousteau's autobiography, called Man, Octopus and Orchid.

Glossary

admiral The commander of a navy fleet

allies Countries that are friendly with each other

ammunition Weapons

amputate To surgically remove a body part

compressed Tightly packed

coral reefs Ocean structures made from the skeletons of sea animals

depth How deep something is

engineer Someone who uses science to solve problems

global warming The gradual warming of Earth's temperatures caused by pollution

mines Places where minerals are extracted from the ground

modified Changed to suit a purpose

mouthpiece A part that goes into the mouth and supplies oxygen

nuclear waste Dangerous chemicals left over from nuclear processes

occupation The control of a country using military power

oil drilling A method of extracting oil from beneath the ground

pressure The weight or force that pushes on something

radar A system that uses radio waves bouncing off objects to determine location

regulator A device that changes air pressure to a lower level

sonar Sound waves used to determine the location of objects under water

submersible A small underwater vessel

undermine To sabotage or destroy

United Nations An organization of countries that works toward world peace

World War II A series of battles that took place between 1939 and 1945, after Germany began invading other European countries to expand its power

Index

Alcyone 23, 27

Antarctica 19, 31

Aqua-Lung 4, 5, 6, 11, 12, 13, 14, 21, 28

awards/honors 15, 19, 29

bathysphere 7

books 4, 5, 17, 31

Calypso 5, 16, 17, 20, 24, 25, 26, 27

Charrier, Bertrand 23

Conshelf 21, 22, 24

Cousteau family 8, 10-11, 16, 19, 24, 28, 30

Cousteau Society 18, 30

crew 11, 24, 25, 26

Denise 22, 23

diving 6, 8, 10, 12, 13, 14, 15, 20, 21, 26

Dumas, Frederic 10, 12, 14, 16, 26

environmental concerns 4, 17, 18-19, 23, 28, 30, 31

Falco, Albert 21, 26

Felix 26, 27

films/filmmaking 4, 8, 10, 12, 14, 17, 20, 21, 26, 28, 29, 30, 31

French Navy 5, 8, 9, 12, 14, 16

Gagnon, Emile 12, 26

inventions 4, 12, 13, 20-23, 28

Malavard, Lucien 23

Malle, Louis 17, 26

Marden, Luis 20

ocean animals 6, 7, 10, 17, 18, 19, 28, 31

Sea Fleas 22

seafood recipe 25

shipwrecks 12, 16

Tailliez, Philippe 10, 12, 14, 26

television shows 4, 31

Thomson, Charles Wyville 6

Turbosail 23

Wesly, Claude 21

World War II 9, 12, 14, 15, 27

Printed in the U.S.A.